Infinite Morning

Infinite Morning

Meredith Carson

OHIO UNIVERSITY PRESS

ATHENS

Ohio University Press, Athens, Ohio 45701
© 1997 by Meredith Carson
Printed in the United States of America

Ohio University Press books are printed on acid-free paper ⊗ ™

01 00 99 98 97   5 4 3 2 1

Library of Congress Cataloging-in-Publication Data

Carson, Meredith, 1913–
    Infinite morning / by Meredith Carson.
        p.   cm.
    Poems.
    ISBN 0-8214-1211-6 (alk. paper). — ISBN 0-8214-1212-4 (pbk. :
alk. paper)
    I. Title.
    PS3553.A7677I53   1997
    811'.54—dc21   97-23690
                                                                   CIP

Acknowledgments

The author of this book wishes to express her grateful acknowledgment to the following publications in which some of these poems have appeared, a few in slightly different form:

Archives of the Arts: "The Hemming"; *Bamboo Ridge: A Hawai'i Writers' Journal*: "Dusting Books," "The Letter," "Light," "Maribou Stork," "A Language"; *Blueline Magazine*: "The Green Up"; *Chaminade Literary Review*: "Antique Buttons," "Beach Bottles," "Pre-Columbian Whistle," "Schooling Fish," "Plankton, Jellyfish, Wingèd Sea Snails and Pelagic Worms"; *Chimera Collections*: "The Breakwater"; *Poetry East and West*: "Kole'a"; *Reach of Song: Georgia State Poetry Society*: "The Secretary Bird"; *Hawaiian Review*: "Jellyfish," "Windows"; *Manhattan Poetry Review*: "The Oleander Sphinx Moth"; *The Sandcutters: Arizona State Poetry Society*: "Greece," "The Snake after Shedding"; *Sister Stew: Fiction and Poetry by Women*: "Light," "Dusting Books"; *Kaimana*: "Beach Bottles."

If the poems in this book are mine, their presentation has been made possible by the many hours of guidance from three friends: Cathy Song, Lois-Ann Yamanaka, and Juliet S. Kono, all successful writers. With the diversity of our Hawai'i, we came together to share our lives in poetry.

Dear friends, in the words of a Hawaiian proverb, *E lei no au i ko aloha*—"I will wear your love as a lei." I thank you from my heart.

Mahalo and Aloha to my husband Hamp for his many helpful remarks—"I have a suggestion . . . ," for his encouragement, and for his technical help with the computer.

To all my teachers and friends who listened throughout the years as I learned, and still learn, this art so mutually loved, I am most grateful.

For Hamp

Contents

III

IV

V

I

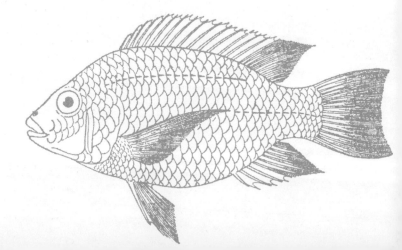

Micro

No planet interests me — too large, too far.
I orbit closer, instead of infinite space,
to infinitesimal, particular —
the world of cell, its living inner place.

I close upon the wilderness of one small leaf
and peer in its green brooks whose brew by sun,
following tissue channels, is pierced in brief
sip of insect. Gravity is undone
by spider web and wing of butterfly.
More power than moon is in the tiny stress
of growth. In micromeasurements there lie
expanded visions bred of earthliness.

Only a bird that leaps from grass and dew
to boundless sky, combines all points of view.

These Plankton, Jellyfish, Wingèd Sea Snails and Pelagic Worms

which scarf their small ghostly bodies
in close consanguinity with water,
are the sea's quiet thoughts
under its rough surface, since
we give the sea our own moods,
which with us too are carried deeper
or upwards by currents.

They pulse, roll with a glitter
of phosphorescent cilia,
coil softly and oar their way towards fate.
All sea's creatures feed upon them,
their glass-clear simplicity
reminding more complex beings
like ourselves
of those sublime sparks of modesty
which preceded us.
Their pale luminous beauty is not
for eyes that want the world's
creatures in full color in six days
following strict rules
of progression.

Some sting
in the invisible trailing way of poetry
that strikes one later,

after pulsating in darkness,
but most feed and delight the hungry
in that middle level where we,
with watery eyes, are submerged
with a wonder where phantom
and reality meet.

Jellyfish

Medusa of the benign curls
cut short and ringed round your flaccid plate,
dessert of the sea turtle
with cream gonad
sitting in your center like a decoration,

you cannot hurt me.

You pulse like a heart
in the sea's breast.
Under the water's bosom
you ride in simple perfection.

I look into your milky mirror
and see myself.
I drip of you;
your cells are mine,
as once within my mother's womb.

I drift with your smooth languor
into Greek waters
of a legendary mind,
full of monsters, whirlpools
and sirens which are dreams.

The Breakwater

Barricade against the long
winter's sea,
this line of huge gray rocks lies
dipping and rising in sea surge
against a continuous sky.
In summers at Provincetown,
when little tides of morning held small menace,
we sat and ran upon it,
squatting near its cave cups where green sea lettuce
floated and tentacles
of pink anemones expanded in the water wind.
We reached down for starfish and waded
safe in a shallow world.

When the sea grew
its rushing of spiral currents,
and came shouldering in,
its stealthy rising
climbed the long shadows of our limbs.
We stopped all play.
The voices of those who called to us
were our own
voices of anxiety.

The scamper and stop of hermit crabs
in their game of no more moving,
the dash and hover of trapped minnows,

the shells of barnacles
clenching around us merged,
as we looked back:
the breakwater deep in our bones.

Pre-Columbian Whistle

This little clay animal with tail curled under,
wearing a hat you blow into,
has a hole under the chin
to let out the piping.

Is it cat, dog, possum,
or the humor of all three?

Costa Rican, it was found
deep in the corner of a tomb,
amid grinding stones and stirrup-spouted vessels,
its little sloe eyes still squinting,
its mouth pursed,
its six holes not yet filled with earth.

My fingers are too wide to play it.
They cover the notes between
so that the thread of a small
tune is broken
and cannot be remembered.

There must be a small child,
to blow it with delight
over and over.

Beach Bottles

My little brother, six, collected bottles,
glass which the sea coughed up.
He'd turn each upside down
to glug the water out.
They held no messages.

Intact as crystal castaways upon the beach,
some clear, some blue or green,
a few, still corked, had dregs like medicine,
a sticky brown.
All had returned as riffraff prodigal
to the material sand their origin.

Those thrown from ships had played the waves,
each bobbling its one eye, then filling, closing it.
Wavering drunk with drink and falling
down and downward to the sea's soft bed,
they tangled in the arms of nets or weeds.
And some were pushed higher by the winter waves
where in the grass and sun
they winked at him until he found them.

After the summers of his childhood tides
they stood, somehow mysterious and hinting.
Later in winters of his wars he left them soldiering.

When the dunes covered them at last
their genii tended him.
His was the emery of sand and wave
whose rubbing set them free.

Death of the Eelgrass

Once in east coast estuaries
it bunched its forests
of green ribbons,
thickets lifting or flattening
in the tides.

It was the nursery of snails,
the mother-skirt of minnows.
The eel's weave parted it.
Crabs clambered through.
Our rowboat floundered, oars draped,
as we eased in our bare feet,
feeling for clams.

Gone. One summer later
the sun stared down on the empty water.
No life moved over the pale sand.
Our feet knew their steps,
while the rowboat was reasonable.

We were not ready for the desolation.
And it was ours.

Schooling Fish

What is the word which their mouths push forward
with such urgency as they breathe
the water into themselves and out,
their eyes transfixed and bright?

Mahimahi, ahi, aku and opelu
move like running stitches
through the dark turquoise
fabric of the tropical sea,
threading their stripes and flashes of iridescence,
and then, in passing, pulling them out,
shifting together in perfect recitation,
having learned their world by rote.

The sea knows their message,
but when the great silent chorus passes
there is no tracing left for reading.

When caught, the mahimahi's color becomes mute.

Carrots

Unlit in the dark
they are what
the blind are told—
lantern-orange.
Pulled up
by their flop-fern
tops, one can
smell their family:
archangel angelica
standing tall,
delicate
caraway, parsley,
Queen Anne,
whose green nests
flatten to lace
doilies of innocent
flowerets,
all with seeds
and roots of crunch.

But mine are mixed up
mandrakes, hairy, with mythical
shriek as I tug,
their sinister toes
and fingers crossing
as if fibbing.
Out of sight

they have been nugget
nudging, titillating
the interstices of my
unrefined soil.

What comes to light is
drawn from the circumstances
of the dark.
It is not easy
underground
for carrots to go
straight, to come up
smoothly as high
ideals of harvest.

Kole'a

The golden plover in his patch of park
stops in his run.
With wire legs and illustrated stance,
breast dark, back brown and yellow speckled,
he watches me.

I am a dark message, an omen.
He has no exorcism, no backward walk,
no counter charm except as a nesting bird,
the trick of broken wing.
This tiny falsehood is no match for mine,
or all my inconsistency.

With straightforward run
he moves from the probe of my stare.

Once more, listening to ground whispers,
his sight is near upon the inch-close worm,
and when he lifts his head he holds,
as if with taxidermy eyes,
an inner vision of some far
tundra now in spring.

As if he waits for his identity
he stands, and then no label holds him.
He rises quickly, curving low.

To him, even my fond eye
stabs him as over the perilous sea
he takes flight.

Annunciation

After a day of dark clouds
and fever of humidity,
an evening sheeted in lightning
and sky pulled across with rain,
the morning lifted blue.

The plumeria tree
left us gifts of fallen petals.
Over and over doves called.
White fairy terns in triplicate,
bits of fluttering,
played round and round the distant
monkeypod tree.

While we awoke there came, it seemed,
a company of angels in the sunlight
formed of our own announcements.

Wings right and left,
those strange redundancies upon each shoulder,
puzzled their arms,
but gave us hope that anything was possible.

This once we believed in them,
the rushing in of those secondary limbs
which bore the messages
of our own revelations.
In all our intemperance of joy
their golden feathers
lifted us.

II

Infinite Morning

Spring with its quiet morning brings
calm water at the beach
with minnows moving in
and people moving seaward.
The waves that lip and brush the sand
invite a transformation.

Far off the swimmers reach their gaze
across that shimmering table
which lays out still for them
their restlessness.

First in the shallows standing,
I watch them inching out
with legs, then waist, and chest
diminishing.

I watch the arms wheel by,
the heads that move
with slow more peaceful
thinking.

I see the rising and the drips,
the shine and then
the steps
into the infinite morning.

Light

The bulbul has flown into the house.
He clings panting to the window curtain,
black crest up and beak open,
his heart racing, black eyes bright.

There is a residue of light
upon his shining feathers.
He showers the air
with bright bird senses.

My house is dark.
Within it I beat as frantically as he,
and so I grasp him,
open my hand and let the sky take him.

Light frees us both and puts us out.
For darkness does not want us.

Those Perishable Things

There were crayfish
down in the springhouse
scudding the soft silt
into thunderheads.

Down through the mowed field
he had followed me.

Dim and cool with the peek of the sun
through the door which hung
on one hinge
and rubbed on mint and grass—

the butter crock, the torso
of the milk bottle
stood in the cold water,
bathers arrested.

"The way we kept them," he said,
"those perishable things."

He stood pool still on the plank,
lingering, keeping past things
in the dark of his heart.
As we left, his eyes closed halfway
like the old springhouse door.

Outside, trickles of tributaries
wound through the grasses,
moved through the meadow,
meeting and blending,
as thoughts in the bask of the summer
are fragile but timeless,
and dragonflies thrusting in air
stitched the light of their wings
to that moment of morning.

Damsel Fly

As if a jeweler
lifted your savage substance
out of the casement of this glass pond
and crafted you,
his hands trembling,
you are at last
split into your transformation.

You alight like a new idea
fragile as surprise,
with iridescent wings
palmed in obeisance to sky.

An emerald pin
clasping a velvet flower,
you impinge upon my sight.
Though you are a gift proffered
and quickly snatched,
memory will hold you.

Indian Pipes

The beech wood startles us
shyly presenting
these little ivory pipes
out of the earth,
for peace, direct from decay.

Their white roots tangle
wildly below dead leaves.
Sometimes called "convulsion root,"
living trees seem to
push them up, as if they were
difficult compromises
after some past evil.
They stand smokeless but waiting,
cold but born of combustion,
and touched with the black scorch
of stem scales which are their leaves.
They look delicately carved from bone.

We never pick them;
they are too close to ghosts
and though beautiful,
we are still troubled.
There are things we can't quite remember,
or don't wish to.

Solitaire

There was no one in the living room
when I came home from school
but a card table which was
Aunt Ida's lap.
Every day above it rose
her purple silk, her white head,
neck in lace choker,
eyes looking down
at the cards' diminishing values
overlapping before her,
as if they were her life's history.

Who was she who never won,
who faced chance quietly, alone,
while I rushed in bleeding?

I heard the soft snap
of the card deck and the steady
ticking of the clock.

The Hemming

Near the old grandmother clock
in the living room
that ticks and pricks the time,
my mother sits hemming
one of the damask napkins
which she purchased for my wedding.
Two edges are in finished selvedge,
but the other two are raw.
Their shadowy leaves and roses interweave
a grace and gentility.

Her stitches, small sand grains,
run through her mind
as through the hours
she hopes to complete me.
I am half peasant, unfinished,
a milk jug of a girl,
checkered in taste,
and set a more casual table.

I watch her small hands at work.
She smooths each piece
across her knee.
The roses of Damascus
shine in the light
out of the soft elegance
of each napkin.
She folds me into the hem with them.

Sand Dollars

Large as my palm or small as a locket,
their coins are all one value
in numismatic whimsy.

Sliding in wave wash far up the beach,
they have the look of alien touchdown.
As they lie bleaching in the sun
with pinched ghosts fled,
they are of our world now
as sand salt shakers
faintly etched with five-part logos
delicate as flower petals.

During the soft pedal of my feet
in the dry sand, I lift them with my toes
and with a twist of wrist, pay their admission
to the wind, spinning them
in a brief new journey.

Greece

Sometimes the air is
as clear as missing arms of statues,
the water as transparent,
making acute our vision.

The hard structure of the land,
with twisted olive trees
clutching at stony hillsides,
tires the pilgrim, yet delights him
with scarlet poppies in goat-cropped fields,
vineyards, and village taverns
with shade and little tables.

White bee boxes are set near
banks of fragrant thyme,
gorges have sacred springs,
grottoes and Pan shadows.

So often earthquake shaken,
the old and new lie broken together.

Here half-invisible temples,
columns of marble
pushed against the sky,
are in our minds made whole,
and old worlds in fragment
can make clear our own.

Persephone

"Won't sad music upset her?"
I asked her frosty attendants.
"She would not
be here if it did," they said.
So my record player spun
music into her revolving day:
allegros of dance,
parades with blue sky and flags,
folk tunes of longing and sadness,
storms at sea.

These were not yet of her world.
She heard only the primitive
plainchant of her fears.

One day as warm winds blew
she awoke to the sounds of harmony,
the scherzo of seeds sprouting above,
the interplay of running roots,
the full orchestration of Spring.

She ran to the sea, listened to it,
and leaning over as one who feels a forehead,
found it well.

Spring Green Up

He rides a tired, common horse,
intentions sitting like stone
within his head. He will
char the land's bone
with fire, to bring the green up.

Dogwood is at his shoulder, redbud,
the white hawthorn, sum
of early spring's dry Ozark
highlands. It's come:
this year is good for burning.

Pieces of clothesline frayed, soaked
in kerosene, lit,
thrown behind in the litter
of oak leaves may benefit
by the new grass, his cattle.

Like the land his weathered
face is scrabbled, its hurt turned
inward. The hills brother
him. With them he's earned
poverty, with humus lost.

Though wrong it seems a right dream
for spring in the bare weather.
He understands abuse and custom.
Here they go together.
For him joy is green up.

Erythrina Seasons

After long seasons of war,
when blood darkens upon the ground,
and the ruins of cities claw towards the sky,
the erythrina trees in February
bloom for us a protest.

The fingers of their red buds
push out and curve towards the earth
as if to clutch it. Later
bouquets are held to the blue sky
amid leafless branches.
They flag hope's passion.

Red petals splash down,
shine on the brown earth.
They lie folded in half lengthwise
like Shinto prayer papers wind-fallen.

Under summer's green ease of leaf
with its canopies of peace,
they will darken, disappear under foot
as blood does in the dust of cities.

III

Dusting Books

Three bearded brothers on a bench
confront me as I am dusting books.
All in their sixties
this eighteen-ninety photograph
was taken by some knickered nephew.
Black business suits, stiff collars,
three gold watch chains swagged across
three paunches, three thumbs
hooked in three watch pockets,
ready to pull the time
in Boston, Brooklyn or Connecticut.

Joseph, Nathan, Allan.
Their ghosts now rise to censure me.
For they collected books.

Believing that excellence of mind in words
deserved raiment that matched,
they bought them in morocco and parchment.
Each limited edition,
numbered in ink, had type articulate.
Wide margins cushioned vision.
Delicate and detailed engravings
were tissued over, veiled as if seraphic.
Gold, like the visible voices of angels,
announced their titles like virgin births.
One believed before one read.

Each set, a living choir,
proclaimed some bright dominion
which they hoped to leave to their descendants,
full of such eloquence and travel
that no one could stay at home.

Through glittering dust in shafts of sun,
they trail my reading eyes.
With my quick turning of a page they sigh together.
The volumes with the broken spines
lean as on ghostly cheeks.
Paper strips like fingers rest in pages.
Volumes are sick with pox and yellowing.
Where are the missing ones?

I dust and sneeze.
I take each volume down.
My own watch ticks with modern certainty.
I will never read them.

Antique Buttons

Old woman sits
cold at her kitchen table,
sorting a spill of buttons,
a threaded needle
ready in her lips.

The cold trout stream outside
talks to itself and in
the glass cabinet the collected
teacups, each hung from one ear,
listen.

Moon discs
of pearl, large,
small, perforated two
times or four, dropped
from garments of persons
now long dead—
a tiny button from a christening dress,
a pewter circle stamped with flower,
a rhinestone trifle winking vanity,
brass piece with anchor from her navy son,
small ivory buckle now illegal,
a white ceramic chunk with stem,
painted with daisy by a friend.

She fumbles through
the lot. Any will do

to keep her rags drawn
close. Their mini-bits
lost and refound,
sewn back,
will warm her.

She chooses one,
a golden ball which fell
as one word fell,
unmatched
forever.

The Snake after Shedding

I saw his skin first,
peeled like a ribbed sock
turned inside out,
lying between two rocks
which had helped him pull.
Fragile as ash,
it was his ghost
on the wrong side of his life
with all its analogues
of scales and tapered grace.

I saw him alive,
smooth and renewed.
Not with the wind
was the grass adjusted!

Threading his way between
the pale dry stems,
his tongue constantly seeking,
he pulled his body's stripe
silent as a secret.

He vanished then
as if his tape spooled up
within root darkness

as I stood without moving
by the delicate wrapping,
of his little gift of fear.

Maribou Stork

There must be hands somewhere,
tucked under these short wings,
and a dirty collar into which
the coarse crumpled neck is sunk.
If not, it is the same poised avarice
of a profiteer hunched four feet tall.

There must be a lock on the legs
for they hold the body's bundle
and thick sword bill
upright as two knobbed,
skinny sticks.

The African servant
came out from the kitchen
with bones and scraps on a plate;
he flung them and the thing
galloped. The bill lunged
securing everything,
while the neck, like a long sock,
flopped and made coughing motions.

I've seen this stalking nightmare
clamber and balance on bushes
as on a soft bedspring and
tweeze out baby birds from their nests,
swallowing them with
one tossed head gulp.

So much of nature is improbable
because the logic evades us,
and macabre because of disturbing
human references.

The Oleander Sphinx Moth

Its chrysalid lay naked by my door,
big as my middle finger, a brown cigar
misplaced, twitching, and though compositor
of its own body, still somnambular.
Days passed, and then it split within my jar
like Heaven opening; dusky dark its eyes,
each wing striped black on tender green with bar
of lavender. It hummed as if in guise
of a tiny bird, hovered, then flung itself at moonrise.

Spider Nights

There is a galaxy of spider eyes
on the night jungle path, inverted
firmament, reflections from my flashlight's beam.

The darkness is acute with senses,
a time of hunting, when childhood
fears spread out before us.

By day they hide as deep as reason,
but wait for us at night, emerging
to halt our journey.

They are so small that seem so large,
these spider nights with tiny worlds
far from our understanding.

A Language

I have been practicing within myself
the voice of my mother
who has been dead for fifty years.
I have been afraid to lose it.
The doves in the early morning
call from their throats:
"We do yes, oh we do yes,"
but their tongues have not spoken.
This wild wolf howling in me
is the world crying. Too great a sound
overpowers meaning.
When I listen to my mother's voice
I hear my name spoken,
all inflections perfect
as in a language
when subtleties are understood
and give solace if repeated softly.

Bonsai

Shorten your years, small tree,
to hasten your trainer's pleasure
and he will prune you like a poem.
He will give rain and food
and treat you as his own,
endangered.

As if you were a book
he will make a delectus
in his mind's journal of forms
which most delight him,
as poets select and trim,
and of those roots and branches of your life
make précis of your growth and story.

You will be insight
when the outside world is far,
or needs a focus,
for your reduction
magnifies, and shows us close
how nature's hand attends
its large exhibits.

Peregrine Falcon

How steady the wind holds him
                              on its fist
as he glides high in the morning sun, watching
the town below,
                    the ships in harbor,
as if he knew
                    small lives could never dodge him.
We've spotted him with all
the excitement of those who see
celebrity.
The King's bird, no, the King himself
whose hard pronouncements have struck
blood.
We watch him quietly,   knowing
him as if we were
his prey.
We've heard his stoop,   rushing through years.
His choice will soon strike hard upon us.
Thus, cleanly given, death tumbles
                              small bird dreams, feathering
the air, and we like them go falling
                              falling,
                              plucked from sky
and brought to earth
where we belong.

My Love Is a Scientist

yet like a fisherman
with no sea before him,
he looks far over the restless and salty
surface of my questions.

He holds the nature of nature telescoped in his eye.
With one spark of evidence leaping
the joy is like the wheeling of birds diving.
He goes and anchors there;
that is the momentary place.

Into the chasms
where pass
the schoolings of the knowable
he hangs his line.
Into places sensed darkly
for that one small tug not yet
captured, he fishes.
He gives me no hearsay.

At last, won by his sight of the right
place, and the patience of fishermen,
his reply is one small catch,
pulled from its place
in the weavings of all earth's life,
given as transient answer.

IV

The Secretary Bird

As if there were needed
a scribe who could not write,
but could bridge thoughtfully
and with vanity
the cold age of dinosaurs
and the warm age of birds,
there came
stalking over the African plain
the Secretary Bird.

Feather-knickered on tall thighs
as if in black velvet,
with classic affectation,
his long tail protrudes
back like a sword
from under black wings and gray waistcoat.

A terrestrial hawk,
he is not interested in sky,
but with red eyes down
searches for snakes.
With feather writing quills
swept behind ear holes
and partly lifted, he is
ready for a stamp and scuffle,
as frantic as a scribbler attacks a page.

As if there were needed
a creature with confidence,
impervious to venom,
feeling both hot and cold,
and passionate with intention,
there came the Secretary Bird,
a creature of dictionary picture,
mannered as a writer
who cannot write.

The Fundamentalist

Under closed lids, like orange
sight, conviction
flickered its lava pools,
and pressured him for power.

He sorted the seen
unseen, and known
unknown, selected them, took
some to fit his certainty.

Slowly his shift and shake caused
him to crack a molten
fountaining which rolled him forth with message.
Time designed, he thought,
and shore extended
would make it rigid.

But lava cools like words and crumbles.
Upon its bed can rise
the question marks of ferns
with truths more fundamental.

Miss Birdseye

Like passages in my music memory,
she still repeats herself,
this teacher of a child
of little talent.

Dressed in perpetual brown
with high-heeled button shoes,
her hennaed hair
gone wrong as her pupils' intonations,
she minced along our street
carrying her violin in its curvy case
and smoking as she went.

The dogs all knew her, barked, and rushed her.
A neighbor called, "Your teacher's here.
She's terrified. Please come and get her."
My father called her "Birdlegs" out of hearing.
I thought she was related
to the frozen peas.

She was convinced her pupils
all were talented.
She suffered with me in duets,
her nicotine-stained fingers patiently
repeating some tiny phrase.
She made me lean to sounds
as children bend over a storyteller.

I am still listening.

One day after a last lesson,
she left me,
clicking down the street like notes diminishing,
and all my practicing departed also,
'til it was heard no more.

Now in the curious moments of my music
mind she has her requiem.

Feral World

Now that the rains are over
the feral cats are out,
establishing their scent again,
rubbing their cheeks along the grass,
squatting to mark new territories.

On the rock couches
near their ghetto holes
along the breakwater,
they sun themselves
and watch the yachts go by
sliding and silken
as life's old purrings and minced meals
that some of them used to know.
Sometimes they lick
the meat of memory as if it clinged to paws,
or they approach with care
the tiny salmon tins left with their dabs
of human caring.

Glaring from under bushes they crouch,
staring suspiciously with marble eyes
at life's betrayal.
They lie down near the path
and then rise quickly,
uneasy, as if they knew
the place was wrong.

But when the gates are shut
and people leave,
dusk gives them muscle.
They creep into the dove-filled lawn
and practice wild meat watching,
lion large.

Dandelions

Every summer the dandelions waited for us—
great prides,
a million yellow heads amid the grass.

We had been waiting also,
each Cinderella
sitting beside the gray hearth of the city,
until we leaped aboard the summer
which took us to our dancing.

Then all our pauper hands turned miser,
clutching limp stems and golden heads
which draped our fists.

But father's voice called down the midnight:
"What terrible dandelions!
What work to save the lawn!"

Rank on rank the mower cut them
and all the lawn grew dark.

The seeds sailed on
and we that sailed them
remained behind
to sit again and dream near winter mice.

Toad

In one of day's night-corners
Bufo, among the garden tools,
is sleeping—
      behind the leaning stack
      of flower pots
      and soggy compost sack.
      He fits in cup of earth
      as in a pudding mold,
      toad fingers circling chest,
      his plump thighs tucked and cold
      against his belly's dough,
      his mouth without a chin
      held low, his eyes half shut.
      In studded-leather skin,
      he's quiet as growth of mildew.

Don't wake him yet.
Shy, in night corners there are some
who wait like him.

Journey

for John-John

What landscape travels you
as you escape yet reach for us?
What hidden tributaries
pull you from cataract to calm,
through maps we cannot read?

Your trails, to us so full of imaginary places
but with your private knowing,
are laid through latitudes of meadow,
longitudes of trees, and drawn like early maps
worn with both fear and yearning,
each marked with talisman of name
familiar yet distant.

These names ahead
await a transformation into
father,   mother.
During your journey
you will hear them nearer, nearer.
That you can speak to them and know them
will be your destination.

The Glass Jar

The hawk moth caterpillar
had been wandering, searching,
when I found it,
its rubber feet
carrying its long gut body
fat and juiced with leaves.

Imprisoned in the jar,
the worm,
soft, obedient to itself alone,
searched like a blind thing, groping,
the sequences of all its beings
stopped.

Imprisoned in deceptions
which long had captured me,
I held my eye upon it, inwardly,
until the glass grew dark.

Then, to better see myself,
I set it free.

The Potter Wasp

When feeling an urgency
for something valuable
to feed our growing image,
we cannot meet this better
than the potter wasp.
Her delicate artistry chambers it
within an urn, fashioned of clay
pressed by saliva kiss
(unsentimental as all instinct).

A slumbering caterpillar, whose bundle
holds her sting of avarice,
as does all garnered treasure,
will feed her pearly egg
for which she labors.

Her perfect pot built round and round
with daubs of dividend to keep it safe
is given extra beauty by a molded neck
to guide the treasure in, a touch
of elegance.

Her gift to growing progeny
and future heritage
is fragile

as in the loss of little things
when poverty is ours.

Ghost Crabs

Ghost crabs haunt the quick and the dead
on the beach's white sea yard.
Some shovel deep,
piling a tumulus
whose only floor is basement.

Bone hard, they box themselves
back in their dark crypts,
lay back their black spook eyes
and sleep,
or listen.

No midnight clock summons them.
Ghost time is when I see each standing
as on four fixed wickets,
watching me;
or it is when the sea bowls towards them,
or my eyes roll momentarily away.
Then they become blown gauze
upon wet bubble-winking sand.

If I lie like one in death,
I have seen them slip out sideways
as pale as sheets of sand.
They skitter on leg multiples
and pick with their chopstick arms
at the small bits which are washed out
by the waves' foam.

If I become alive
their tall eyes are all-seeing.
They vanish
to wait entombed, listening
'til the long limbo of my patience
reassures them.

V

Connections

Each part of earth needs touch
of bird feet, small seed, insect,
like words, looks, promises,
to drop upon it lightly, both
small exotica
and things it knows.

My mind needs landings
in notes of music,
curious postcards of foreign places,
in friends to keep accepting
my weathers and my weatherings.

Each shore needs landfall,
small points settling down,
like mangrove sprouts
floating, wobbling vertically
like pencils in the sea.

White Waters

lifting in the sea
are the sea's voice,
yet all its breaking in
speaks superficially.

You are beside me on the beach.
Your words come to me,
evasive as sliding surf,
approximate, then out of reach.

Black currents deep below
are quiet. I plumb
what seems as incomplete
as luminous lines of fish that go

partly unseen and partly glowing.
If I could catch what is below the tumult
I would complete my knowing.

Windows

To the bird that enters the house
and flies against glass,
the window lies.
His truth is the sky.

When I am halted by such hard shining,
with vision selected of earth,
framed in the sun or rain,
prismatic, wonderful,
I can have insight into what is without,
outfly the bird
to what the bird knows.

The Mower of Grass

knows only the level of his head,
the shooter of hawks his skies.
Men have their measurements.
But there are none of them
the hawk can use.
He has his own, unnamed,
within the window of his sky.

So many senses engineer
to give the eye its focus
that all the windows to the earth,
both high and low, become,
with all their ways of measurement,
infinity itself.

Picture Album

Star bright faces.
Twenty years have been light years.
Only now have they reached me.
Many faces have died, but are still shining.
There are lesser stars which stand behind
half hidden, not yet named.

I have opened the shutter of its window.

In the clear night
when one is farthest from others,
I count the years and
wonder, after the motionless
moments of each picture,
what is myth and what real
in the motion of these lives,
and what, even now,
pulses in the dark space between us.

Walking on Kilauea's Lava

Sitting on the fire beneath us,
earth's cooled kettles crack
where we dare not walk,
turning pot to melt,
then back to flame,
present back to beginning.

We tread carefully
as life which tests its walk,
its leap, its crawl,
and drop each foot like seed
upon the cooling of this heave and split,
these bulbous pillows.

Small mats of flowers, quick ferns appear
along our perilous route
as if they were, like us,
eager to place their kind early
before the rise of mountains.

The sinking of the sun's round
fire chills the day
and liquid flame arises.
Upon this warm yet razor skin
we balance.

After Grandmother's House Burned Down

Black as negative the house
lay piled and crisp,
like fist of jackstraws dropped,
lying as if with gentle touch
dark memories would tumble.
The family, ghosted so long ago,
seemed in my mind reversed
and dark as the transparencies of photographs.

In my mind's positive
I saw the white frame mansion with veranda
handsome and freshly painted,
a child with golden hair,
proper in buttons and white pinafore,
building castles in a sand box
under an apple tree,
a garden with larkspur and pink roses,
and grandma with a basket,
a birthday party.

No death or pain, no secret tragedy.
Each in the family gathering smiled.

This could not be without a negative,
for all years have their burning.

Time's Tributary

At dusk,
over the muddy water
of an Orinoco tributary
    small bats zigzag
    through the dust of gnats.

My boat
moves through
the scent of flowers
whose distillation
powers the night with longing.

    On either side
    the green forest of wading trees
        hangs over
    the deep passage.

With rain and moon
there is both darkness and shine.

I float
between the years
through an opening and closing
    of their light
when I pulled my boat shallow
through a river of mourning,
a river of salt.

The bats
with their wire feet
unstaple themselves
from the leaning trunks.

They scatter in all directions
as notes
or jottings
on torn scraps of paper.

The Letter

Far off, yet closer by years
to his dying, it has come in a letter,
the voice of my father:
"Glad you are coming home."
At last in the climb of his age
he has reached me.

Backwards I look into childhood
down that mountain, that stairwell
where he followed my spiraling
upwards and upwards, laboring,
throwing the rope of his anger,
casting and failing,

a stranger, mounting behind me,
clumsy and heavy of step,
struggling for help but not asking,
while I ran on before him,
alone, dreaming, backpacking guilt.

Now in this letter he cloud walks,
lifted and smiling,
smooth and forgiving,
brushing me gently
as paper, fluttering paper.

Banyan Tree

I came to its circus
for a penny moment
and looked up into its tent
which wind-wallowed
against the sky.

With a steady gaze
I balanced high
with the inhabitants of its nimble world,
watching the glint of birds practicing.

Under the perpetual
summer of its green and shadowed leaves,
I moved in memory
around the wide circumference of my years,
leaping backwards and forwards
as in dreams,
always with skill,
never failing.

From the old tree's ramps and struts,
root bundles hung like ropes.
I grasped them to my breast,
and taking the tree's own strength
and the dream's disguise,
prepared once more to swing.

Centuries of Being

Over a river edged with bullrushes
this summer's cliff swallows
fling their black bodies,
sharp chips of feather,
across a canyon sky,
hundreds leaving, returning
from mud nests bracketed against
a cliff of lava.

They will go south soon,
emptying the air of chatter,
leaving a vacancy for the cold wind
along these ancient flanks of cataclysm.

But spring will find them once again
flying above the river's
momentary mirror,
all fragile and yet sure
within their centuries of being swallows,
each tweezer beak
fetching and placing
its mite of mortar.

Mauna Kea Summit

This mountain
higher than Everest,
if measured from the sea's black floor,
pushes its glittering grit of cinder cones
as if it knew monastic solitude.
Instead, a science citadel looks up with vision faceted.

Moving slowly in height,
our separate bodies cautious,
we learned at last
that Heaven is tiredness
while Earth is easy.

The white light and purity of snow
that winter, poured its whole prism
like sacrament into our mortal eyes.

Tall candles of mullein plants
along the rocky road
could not warm us
as our breathing toiled upwards.

Only this clear and infinite level
of our strivings
seemed real.
Earth seemed of less account
than our new shining.

Soon in the cold,
we asked in heresy to return,
and bent our longing homeward.

Then Earth rose up to meet us
as we descended,
so that instead we shone
in its rich oxygen.

Pianissimo and Crescendo

Long ago it was quieter.
Bees went round and round gazebos,
larks spiraled over little fields
in which the drama
of the summer seasons played
long and slowly,
while hedgerows of birds and rabbits,
like children at a matinee,
fidgeted, left and were re-seated.

Lovers bent close
and twenty-six-string lutes,
encircled by each player's inner arm,
were pressed against their hearts,
and two together listened.

Now into the vast arena of the sky
the radar bowls uptip to catch
some distant drop of word,
and the electric strings
and microphones in fists
now amplify at any season.

The birds have vanished note by note,
and lutes lie broken.
Give me a message on a small cassette
to prove that we have spoken.